Love It or Leave It

The End of Government as the Problem

Mark Manney

For Sofia and Isabella.

CONTENTS

1 FREEDOM FROM GOVERNMENT

Do you believe that government is the problem? Do you believe in the free market? Do you believe in freedom? Do you want the government off your back? I have a question that each of us needs to answer: **If you were offered the chance at total freedom from taxes and total freedom from government in your life, would you take it?**

A bullet-proof and realistic argument can be made that this should become a real option for every American. But first, you should know that this book *is not* what you probably think it is. This is not about me trying to convince you that I am right and you are wrong. It is not an argument about anything that is theoretical or abstract. I don't care about debating whose ideas are right or whose are wrong. I'm bored with it. You weren't born yesterday and you already know what your beliefs are. Who am I to try to convince you to change anything? Why would I even want to?

Instead, let's talk about *reality* for a change. Despite all of the well-reasoned, yet abstract, political debates of the past few decades, ideas are only interesting or meaningful when they have something to do with the *actual reality* that we *actually experience* in our *actual lives*. Ideas, arguments, and debates mean almost nothing when they are either unrealistic or are so pure that they have little relevance to the way the world actually works. What about reality? When *I say* the word "reality", I'm talking about the reality that each of us knows *in our own lives*…what we actually do, see, experience, and feel.

But big ideas are also important because sometimes they affect reality. Here's one big idea that has shaped the world over the past 35 years:

"The nine most terrifying words in the English language are, 'I'm from the government and I'm here to help.'"

-Ronald Reagan, future US President, 1975

Does this statement ring true to you? This way of thinking has become so much a part of our lives that I probably don't even have to explain what Ronald Reagan was talking about. We know that he was talking about the evils of government and the benefits of free-market economics. Any student of Econ. 101 or any American citizen paying any attention to the news or to political talk-shows over the past few decades can explain the conventional wisdom about the benefits of laissez-faire, free market economics.

It isn't even necessary to explain the invisible hand of supply and demand; how, in the absence of any external control or intervention, market forces will naturally set the right prices and ensure that the right amounts of the right goods are produced. There is absolutely no reason for me to spend much time explaining the idea that the market is capable of solving all problems. The same forces which work so well at the grocery store, at the mall, or at the farmer's market should certainly work the same way when it comes to the labor market, healthcare, transportation, education, and every aspect of modern life. That's how the theory goes, right? The market is self-correcting and solves all problems.

This way of thinking was introduced long ago by Adam Smith and was, more recently, revived by Milton Friedman. In the 1950's, Friedman started the modern-day free market economics movement at the University of Chicago's Economics Department. At the time, his ideas were considered extreme and radical. Today they are completely in the mainstream. Indeed, the ideas behind this "Chicago School Economics" movement have been spread to nearly every part of the planet and are now inseparable from most modern political thought.

If we do, in fact, believe that the free market is perfect and solves all problems, we also know what prevents the free-market system from working in the way that it should. Ronald Reagan alluded to the answer to this question in the above quote: *government*. Government messes up the perfect functioning of the free market by (among other ways) establishing minimum wages, workers rights, retirement pensions, healthcare programs, and even public schools. Government controls the money supply, establishes laws restricting free trade, tries to control monopolies, and levies taxes (which unnaturally redistribute wealth). The ultimate goal is a laissez-faire government that does not influence or control the economy. In the simplest terms, if we want things to "work properly", then *less government is always the goal*. All of what appears to be a failure in the market is really just a sign that the government has interfered in the free market and the situation could easily be remedied if the government would just stop interfering.

One wouldn't have to make too large of a leap to conclude the obvious: that if government is indeed the problem, then the role of government should be minimized or even completely eliminated from our economy and from our lives. Conservatives since Reagan have run for office on this message. Interestingly, supporters of these conservative, right-wing, or libertarian politicians are not actually voting to put someone in government who is there to represent their best interests *through the mechanism of government*. Instead, supporters of these politicians actually hope that their guy or gal gets elected to *undermine* and to *destroy*

3

government. Many of their supporters believe that the extent to which these politicians are able to destroy or undermine government, itself, is the extent to which they are indirectly *helping us* by letting the free market work as it should.

I offer this background not to educate you, the reader. I only wanted to point out that *I get it*. I get the argument put forth by Friedman, by his followers, and by conservatives of all sorts…but especially self-identified Republicans, Libertarians, and anybody who sympathizes with the Tea Party movement. But, as I mentioned, this book is not so much about theoretical ideas as it is about *reality*. It isn't really possible for anyone to talk about reality without bringing his own, personal perspective that has come about as a result of his own life experiences. But every attempt will be made to force myself outside of my bubble, to think long and hard about the different kinds of people I've known, and to think about the lives I've observed in all of the communities I have been a part of.

I grew up on an all-American diet with healthy helpings of strong family values, religion, and the kind of patriotism that could only come from The Heartland of America (central Wisconsin, to be exact). I guess my family was lower-middle class. My parents couldn't afford to help me pay for college, so my dad always told me that the only way I could afford to go to University was to become good enough at basketball (a sport I was pretty good at) to earn a scholarship. I practiced basketball practically every day, at least two hours a day, year-round from 7th grade until I graduated High School. Just as my dad had hoped, on a basketball scholarship I managed to find my way into University to study Business. I earned my Bachelor's in Marketing and then earned an MBA in Technology Management from the University of Colorado. I now have more than 15 years of experience working for some of the most successful (and unfortunately for me even a few unsuccessful) corporations.

So first of all, I get it: business is a good thing. It provides us with jobs that make the American Dream possible. How could we even begin to imagine our individual pursuit of happiness without profit-seeking business? We all need money to live and landing a job working for a successful business seems like a pretty good way to get it. I also owe a lot to greed. Now I work in Sales. I get my share only when the investor earns more from my work than I am paid. If I'm being honest, I can also tell you that sometimes I hate being taxed because it feels like the government has no right to take hard-earned money from my pocket and spend it in the endless ways that I don't agree with. Basically, I feel like there's nothing wrong with having money if it is earned in an honest way.

I tell you this only to explain that I've been there, done that, and like most of America I am frustrated by what I see happening these days. In this book, I will take the ideas I believe we, as Americans, hold most dear and do my best to carry them *all the way through to reality*. I will do this by discussing the big question asked at the start of the book. I will then propose a specific Act of Congress to put this idea into action. This is an idea that will change everything!

2 WHAT DO YOU MEAN "LOVE IT OR LEAVE IT"?

I guess every American President tells us that we are all united because we are all Americans. They tell us that, while we may have our differences, what matters most is that we are all Americans. What exactly does it mean to be an American? What are some of the values that each and every one of us share?

Americans think differently than people in other countries. If we are true American patriots, it seems that most of us believe that our thinking should go something like this:

1) Capitalism (or the free market) is the source of all wealth and prosperity and solves all problems as long as it is not interfered with, and

2) American Democracy, based on the Constitution, is the most perfect form of government the world has ever seen, and

3) *Even if* America isn't always perfect, if we are hard-working and self-reliant enough, we all have a shot at the American Dream (which is something completely unique to America), and

4) If you have any fundamental questions or doubts concerning points 1 – 3, then you are not truly American and, as the saying goes, you can "love it or leave it."

Isn't this at least part of what we mean when we talk about the idea of being a "true American"? Here's the problem I have: there isn't an American alive who will not have some kind of fundamental problem with at least some of these points! I would argue that I don't know if anyone can actually get to the "love it" part anymore! Please, don't get worked-up. I'm on your side. I am not anti-American and nothing I will say should offend you. Please allow me to continue.

As I said, the first point is that the free market is the source of all wealth and prosperity and it solves all problems as long as it is not interfered with. Liberals would argue that the market *does not* actually take care of everything. The market does some things perfectly well, but other functions (like building roads, managing social programs to fight poverty, providing law enforcement, fire departments, defense, the legal system, etc.) are best left to the government. Furthermore, the trouble Liberals have with leaving everything up to the market is the issue of social justice. They feel that, in the Judeo-Christian tradition, it is moral and right to help the poor and the less fortunate. They don't believe that charity, alone, is enough to make sure that no single person is left behind to suffer, die of starvation, or freeze in the cold in hopeless poverty. They believe that, in a prosperous country, it is an acceptable and necessary sacrifice for all of us to pay enough in taxes so that we can make sure that life is less brutal and short for the less fortunate among us.

Liberals also believe that the government has a big role in creating a strong middle-class. This is done, in part, by ensuring equal opportunity for every child. The market does not provide equal opportunity by itself (it naturally favors the already-rich because money buys more opportunity and some people are born rich). So they believe, in short, in a social safety-net and in equal opportunity. These people object to the very premise of the idea that the free market is the source of *all* wealth and prosperity and solves all problems as long as it is not interfered with.

On the flip side, true believers in free market economics actually object to this idea on entirely different grounds. While they may believe *the idea* is correct, they still cannot get to the "America, love it" part because the US government clearly is *not adhering to the idea.* They feel as though the government is too socialist, that it taxes too much and spends too much on wasteful and ineffective social programs. They see that the government puts far too much regulation on business (minimum wage laws, a complicated tax system, regulations about hiring and firing, safety regulations, sales taxes, licensing, etc., etc.). They might even notice that the current economic system in the US looks more like a rigged market than a free market. The government seems to be mostly just taking care of big finance, big oil, big auto, big defense, big insurance, big, big, big. The government sets up policies which basically ensure that true competition never actually happens, that the already large and powerful corporations maintain their favored and protected status while the small business owner stands no real chance to compete on a level playing-field. This isn't exactly Capitalism we're talking about, is it?

So how exactly are we supposed to all be united under this "capitalist ideal" when pure Capitalism doesn't actually exist in the USA and, even if it did, a large portion of the country doesn't share the ideal anyway? Regardless of which side of this argument you are on, both of these opinions must be recognized simply because they are the honest beliefs and observations of *real people.* "Love it or leave it", they say, huh?

If you favor a Liberal state of true equal opportunity, social justice, and a social safety-net, you cannot *love* the fact that children are not guaranteed even healthcare when they are sick. You cannot *love* the fact that University is becoming so expensive that it is only available to wealthier individuals (or those with athletic abilities). If this is your belief system, you are correct to fundamentally disagree with the first statement. You might, indeed, have legitimate issues in getting to the "love it" part.

On the other hand, if you are a true believer in the free market ideal, then you are also correct not to *love* that what we have seen in the US over the past 100+ years is not free market capitalism – far from it. As I said, the government *does* interfere all the time with socialist programs and in so many other ways. So if these four points at the start of this chapter are the ways we are going to define what it means to love America, and we already can't love point one, what are we to conclude? But let's go on to the next point.

American Democracy, based on the US Constitution, is the most perfect form of government the world has ever seen, right? There are several ways to interpret this statement. Once again, are we thinking of our government as it actually is, or are we referring to the *idea* of the Constitution? I ask this because, even if we do have complete faith in the Constitution, it might also be noted that the Constitution was not, and is not, always followed perfectly. But if the Constitution is so perfect, then why exactly is it not perfect enough to ensure that it is actually followed? Doesn't the Constitution describe the way our government was supposed to work? How can we, in good faith, say that the system created by the Constitution is not working so well and yet the document is perfect?

Anyway, when I'm talking about US Democracy, I'm talking about US Democracy as it actually exists. These days, Washington just doesn't seem to work. It doesn't seem to get anything done that has any real impact on our real lives. Americans who feel this way might simply not "love it" on the grounds that Washington has just become *bad at governing*.

Perhaps, however, there is a portion of the population that is completely happy with our government as it is. Many business executives and others who can afford to give huge campaign contributions in exchange for favors, or anyone receiving government contracts and selling their products or services to the government is likely quite happy with American Democracy as it currently is. Anyone working for the government is also likely to be quite happy with the status quo. Those in the media (across the board from Jon Stewart to Bill O'Reilly) are probably quite thrilled that the government gives them so much to talk about in such an entertaining way. There might even be a bunch of people at home who actually agree with the direction of our government (though I'm not sure how many of them actually pay enough attention to know the reality about what the government is doing). So let's say these people are, at least, *enjoying the game* of Washington politics.

Now let's talk about the American Dream. Some of us might define the American Dream as working hard, pulling ourselves up by our own boot-straps, owning a home, etc. I think this attitude is very admirable. This is the type of idea that influenced me growing up and this is actually the attitude I have always lived by. However, if I'm being completely honest, I should say that this isn't something unique to America. People work hard, earn lots of money, and own nice homes in many other countries around the world. The chance of getting rich isn't all that much better in the US anymore. The reality is that the US tax rate is about the same as in other countries. Another sad truth is that the US tax system is one of the most complicated in the world. More importantly, I can tell you as a business person, in terms of opportunity, the US is a very mature, saturated market. Just as a practical matter, it is actually a bit *more difficult* to succeed in business in the US because there are fewer untapped opportunities than in other, more emerging markets.

Life can be difficult for entrepreneurs in the US. Not only is the playing-field very competitive, but it can feel like so much is working against you. For example, so many young, would-be entrepreneurs attend college and then end up owing so much in student loan debt that they really don't have the luxury of taking on yet more risk to borrow even more money. Even the most solid business ideas are often crushed under the weight of personal debt, sometimes very early in life. This isn't the case in many other Western countries, where those who qualify for college admission have their university paid for by the government (which eliminates the need for any student loan debt). Also, in the US, entrepreneurs are forced to purchase their own private and very expensive health insurance because they are not working for an employer who would otherwise help provide coverage. This is yet another incentive to stay in a job instead of starting a small business. Connecting health insurance to a job, in fact, is a uniquely American and slightly strange way of providing healthcare. Think of this from the perspective of a business owner. If you do run a successful business and are in a position to hire employees, you end up having to pay the healthcare costs of those employees (on top of all the other taxes in this complicated system). The combination of all of this makes it a bit more challenging, indeed, to become rich through self-sufficiency, hard work, and entrepreneurship in America. It can actually be easier in other countries. I hate to say this, because I know how Americans hate to hear it.

I told you I would be completely honest in this book. Here's a twist you may not have seen coming. After hearing what I have to tell you, you may even feel as though I am not even *as American* as you. I don't say this sarcastically. I'm proof-reading this book again and again to look for, and delete, any sense of sarcasm. Sarcasm is intellectual laziness, snobbery, and elitism. The ideas of this book are too important to denigrate with sarcasm. To mock someone else's beliefs is to demonstrate a complete failure to put oneself in another person's shoes. Anyway, as I was saying, you might think I am not as American as you, the reader. Why?

I am a US Citizen, but I actually have lived outside of the United States during the last few years. I have done this for personal reasons. I happened to have stumbled upon a life that suits me well, at least for the time-being, in Eastern Europe (in a country most people know nothing about – Slovakia). It is a small country in Eastern Europe, part of the EU, and on the Euro currency. I'm also kind of proud to say that I've made this move without really making a sacrifice in terms my career (there's that all-American pride in self-reliance). Anyway, now that you know this about me, please try to hang in there with me as you continue reading. I hope that this book reveals an idea that will redeem me as a true American patriot in your eyes anyway. For now, just know that *I am* an American and I'm on your side!

I bring this up only to compare what I have observed in Europe with the idea of the American Dream. It is a shame, I have to admit it, but even in the tiny country where I now live, I have seen that a person's odds seem better when starting a small business and becoming independently wealthy. That's because here, there is a simple 20% (very low) flat-tax. Healthcare insurance is covered by the government automatically. Your university education is also paid for. On top of this, it is an emerging market still with a lot of untapped potential for hard-working individuals with good ideas. Even if you should fail (which most businesses do no matter how great the conditions), well then there's always a reasonably strong social safety net to help you out until you can find a job or give it another go.

What I'm saying is that, if you look at the situation in reality, the only thing unique about America in terms of opportunity is that it is actually *more difficult* to pull yourself up by your own boot-straps and become independently wealthy. That's because so much is working against you in America. Sometimes it feels like we are swimming upstream even when we are being responsible and doing exactly as we are told. It would seem to me that it would make sense to celebrate the fact that your country makes it *more possible* to become rich through hard work, not *less possible*, right?

You could argue that it is probably still a bit more likely to find a higher-paying corporate job in the US than in most other countries (as I have done throughout my career). But I don't think "finding a good job with benefits" has much to do with the original American Dream. Maybe those with a good job and a nice home are perfectly happy, indeed. But, again, I don't see what that has to do with the American Dream. Germans, French, Brits…a huge percentage of Europeans and many Asians also have good jobs, good benefits, nice homes, and a bunch more vacation time than Americans.

What other ideas are associated with the American Dream? Perhaps becoming uber-famous? Well that's also possible anywhere. There's nothing particularly American about it. In fact, it is easier to become famous in a smaller country with less competition because of its smaller pool of talent.

Does any of this, what I've been talking about, actually have anything to do with the American Dream? I just now realized that I haven't even discussed the *real* American Dream! Have you noticed? I bet you sensed that there was something missing, right? If not, that's alright because I only realized it just now too. But ask yourself this: what is the core idea behind the American Dream? It actually isn't *just* the idea of owning a home, becoming rich or becoming famous. Remember? The origin of the American Dream, the idea that inspired all of those brave people to settle the new continent to begin with…it was the idea of *freedom!*

Freedom goes far beyond what I've been talking about. The early American settlers had lost faith that the governments in their countries would change. They felt oppressed by the Church and wanted to practice their own forms of religion. They dreamt of owning a piece of land, of eventually becoming *self-sufficient*. They wanted to be *free from oppression*! This is freedom! The early American settlers simply wanted the freedom to change their own lives for the better. Hundreds of years ago, America provided a real chance at freedom. People understood that they'd be giving up comfort and taking enormous risks. They also knew that there was no going back. But enough people were brave enough that they came anyway, in search of the kind of freedom that was previously unimaginable. It wasn't for everyone, but what mattered is that *it was possible at all.*

Where is that kind of freedom possible now? Not in America, where every citizen gets a Social-Security number so they can track us from birth, where every citizen has to report their income and be taxed each year of their life, where we can't have a beer at age 20 even if we are old enough to shoulder all of life's adult responsibilities, where the government even has the power to take away our children if some bureaucrat doesn't like how we are raising them, where we can't grow a plant at home and smoke it if we choose to do so. Now we're even going to be required, by law, to buy health insurance! We are, indeed, not truly free! I'm not saying there is anywhere else in the world, at least that I know of, where this kind of freedom is entirely possible (though there is a good chance I'm wrong about this). But either way, I wish America could once again become this different kind of place…this place it *wants* to be and *claims* to be!

The good news is that I have a simple, completely realistic idea to restore the possibility of true freedom in America.

3 THE TOTAL FREEDOM ACT

At the beginning of the book, I asked a fundamental question: **If you were offered the chance at total freedom from taxes and total freedom from government in your life, would you take it?**

I am proposing exactly this. I am proposing that Congress and the President pass what I will call the **Total Freedom Act**. Let me introduce the proposed piece of legislation:

- The Total Freedom Act will restore the possibility of complete freedom by offering every American the chance to completely opt-out from paying any taxes.
- In return for the right to live in complete freedom and pay no taxes, citizens who exercise their right to live under the Total Freedom Act cannot benefit at all from the government or from any government program.
- Those living under the protection of the Total Freedom Act will be independent from and untouched by the laws of the United States. The only exception to this is when it comes to those laws that are protecting tax-paying citizens (your right to exercise freedom cannot harm tax-paying citizens).

- Those who have opted to live under the Total Freedom Act but who wish to return to their former status as a tax-paying citizen can only do so by back-paying any taxes that would have been owed during the time spent living under the Act.

The case will be made that the enactment of the Total Freedom Act is something that should be fought for by each and every American. I will also explain why Washington should want us to have this option. As you recall from the previous chapter; the truly *unique, original* aspect of the American Dream – the origin of the idea – is the belief in *true freedom*. Back in the early days of America, when people around the world could no longer tolerate the oppressive country in which they lived, when it seemed as though they had little opportunity, when they desired to be free, they came to America. They weren't guaranteed success on this quest for true freedom; rather, they were promised only that they had *a chance* at freedom.

Even after these early settlers had established themselves in the new world, even if they didn't like how things were going in New England, for example, they were free to go out West, buy some land (or be given some land by the government), and were free to brave the wild frontier in search of that better life. I'm not talking about these settlers in an abstract sense. These were real people, with real feelings, with real hopes, and with real dreams. Sometimes they won big, sometimes they failed badly and fell hard. Other times, they ended up on some quiet, small farm somewhere in Wisconsin, where they had unremarkable children who went on to live unremarkable lives taking over the family farm. Like I did. Just kidding. But they did all of this on their own terms. That's the point. *They were free people exercising free will.* They did not feel like subjects to a monarchy. They did not feel oppressed by big government or by big business. They were free to live and work. They were free to fulfill their dreams or die trying. They were true Americans!

American settlers were also free to go even further west, to California in search of gold perhaps. In each of the towns they passed through, there may or may not have been a sheriff. There may or may not have been law and order. These brave men may or may not have gotten themselves into a gun-fight outside of a saloon to resolve a dispute. They were free to drink hard and even to visit a whorehouse if that is what they wanted to do. Nobody could stop them. They weren't perfect people. This wasn't at all about family values, as the Disney films would have us believe. This was about freedom! *This* was the American Dream. Remember?

We can recognize this same longing for freedom in the voices of people shouting that government is the problem. You want to be free from government? You want to live according to free-market principles? You want to stop paying taxes? You want to be completely free? Perhaps you aren't sure whether you would opt to live in the kind of freedom I'm describing, but maybe you'd at least want to know that there's an option like this *available to you if you want it.* So come along with me as I take our case right to the government.

4 TO THE RULING ELITE

Let me shift tone a bit. Now I'm *not* talking to you, the reader. I'm *not* talking to you – my equal, my fellow American, my friend and neighbor. Let me speak plainly to power. I have a question for you, the selfish, smug, and corrupt elite in power and all of the obscenely wealthy funders who support you. Here it is: people often say "America, love it or leave it." The thing is, you have an important role here. You have a job to do. Maybe you didn't even know this, but actually it *is your job* to make it possible for us to get to the "love it" part! You have the power! You run the country, remember? How are we supposed to love it when you have built up a country that is run by a government that does not get anything done for us or reflect any of our values? How could you have stripped away each of the ideals we hold dear not just as Americans, but as humans, and then ask us to feel like proud Americans? How can you do this without even offering us *the option of freedom*?

This is my idea. This is my request. This is my plea. This is a simple thing that you could do to restore America. I'm not even asking you to give up your power! I'm only asking for you to recognize *my right* to be a free human being. If it isn't too much trouble, you might get around to allowing me the dignity of becoming the rightful owner of my own self! I'm tired of being forced to fight a losing battle in a rigged game. I know that my side will not win. You win! You own the casino and the house *always* wins. Now please, can we have at least *the option* of freedom? Can we have *the option* of walking out the door of the casino when we've had enough?

Why in the hell are you encouraging people who believe in *less government* or *no government* to get involved with the *mechanisms of government*? They want *freedom*! They don't want to become part of your corrupt game! They want to free themselves from government. Get it? You are making a mockery of these people. In your rhetoric, you are dangling a "government is the enemy" carrot out in front of them and laughing at them as they vote for your people and follow your government around the track. But this is a race that you've already rigged on a racetrack that you own. They want you out of their lives! So take a hint! Sometimes it seems like you are some kind of an abusive husband in a horrible marriage. She doesn't need you! She wants you out of her life! Give her some basic level of human dignity and let her be free if she so chooses. It is the right thing to do. That doesn't necessarily mean she's going to leave. Don't be so insecure! Let her have the option so that, if she stays, you know you actually have her loyalty.

I'm asking only for the option to completely opt-out. That means the option to have nothing to do with you. That means the option to pay you no taxes and to submit to none of your laws other than those protecting others who continue as tax-payers. In return, those who choose to live under the Total Freedom Act will not use any of your services. They will not send their children to your schools. They will not drive on your roads. They will not take advantage of your courts. They will not work for any organization receiving any money from the government. They will certainly not ask for unemployment benefits if they lose their jobs. They will not ask for Welfare. They will not expect Medicare or Medicaid in their old age. They will not call the police departments or fire departments during a time of trouble. They will not use the post offices or any other service that is funded by the government.

Should they be allowed to use the dollar as currency? I guess this is a difficult question because the US government did create the dollar. My opinion is that we should allow everyone to still transact business in dollars because, these days, management of the money supply is not really a function of the government anyway (you put this into the hands of the Federal Reserve a long time ago).

People who do choose to live under the Total Freedom Act are fair-minded and will have no intention to take advantage. They simply believe strongly in the power of the free market. Let them live their dream by choosing a life where they are part of a completely free market that the government does not interfere with. Do you not believe in freedom? Do you not believe in the free market as most of you say you do?

If you do allow us this option then you will have to respect that, when individuals choose this option, you will have no right to touch them – these brave and idealistic people who opt-out from paying tax into a system they disagree with and morally oppose. This is a simple exchange: you grant us the possibility of choosing the most real kind of freedom and human dignity. Those who choose this option promise not to demand anything back from you. We cut our ties. Please know that we do understand, and we accept fully, that of course we have no right to demand anything back when we are not paying-in.

There is still more I have to say to those of you in positions of power and influence, those of you who actually do have the power to grant us this request. Why on Earth would you *not* give us this option? Are you afraid that we would actually *use it*? Are you so insecure that the life you offer us, the system *you set up* and force us to submit to, the entire way of life that you have created and fight so hard to maintain…are you really so insecure that we would *choose not to take part in your system*? Then, I ask, what *legitimacy* do you have?

To not allow us the option to opt-out as active citizens and tax-payers is to rule us illegitimately. I thought this was supposed to be a government by consent. Funny, I don't remember formally agreeing, at any moment in my lifetime, that I *do consent*. Do you not think we get adequate return on our tax investment? Your failure to grant us this request can be taken only to mean that you doubt your own value and legitimacy! Just as governments have done throughout the ages, you feel that you have to rule by force. But, in truth, the starting point for democracy is that place where the people understand the value of government, choose to form one, and choose to take part in a system that is legitimate. They do this not out of fear or obedience, but as free, rational people who clearly understand why they *want* government. In doing so, they also have some idea what kind of government they would like to have. Do you not see that Americans are losing this fundamental faith in, even desire for, government itself? Do you not see how the Total Freedom Act can so quickly restore it?

If you haven't noticed, the country is in a state of fundamental crisis. I think it is time to go back to the basics. Give us a choice. Give us the option of freedom. When people say "love it or leave it," give us something to love or give us a real way to leave. For some of us, that option might involve moving abroad to some other country. In that case, I beg you, let us completely opt-out (which we currently can't do) so that we no longer have to report our annual income to the US Government even though we are not living there and not using your services. You require this for the purpose of making us pay double-taxation on anything over $80,000, but what right do you think you have to take anything from me when I earn my money outside of your borders and do not burden you in any way? Let me be. Let me be *free*. Leave me alone!

Others, who do not want to seek a better life in some foreign country, should have the option to do just as I have explained: to opt-out as a taxpayer, to live within America's borders but to be left alone. In return, they will not vote, will not ask anything from you, and will leave you, the government, alone. You may not understand what these people are asking for, but it *isn't your role* to understand it or to decide whether or not this makes any sense for them. Maybe these people simply believe in real freedom, in self-sufficiency, and in independence. Maybe they believe in the free market. Maybe they are crazy…who cares? But why, when the crazy hippies went far off into the mountains on private land to live exactly as they wished and smoked whatever they wished in private, why did you send the police to harass them? Why couldn't you have left them alone? What right did you have to tell them what they could or couldn't do when they weren't harming anybody? And why, in Waco, Texas, when a few people wanted to practice their own religion freely and behind closed doors, why did you attack them with the full force of the military? Stop the abuse! Give us a way to be left alone if we want to be left alone! And please, don't take it personally. These are *our lives* and we live just once. You go on and live your dream and we'll live ours.

5 MY INTERESTS, YOUR INTERESTS, EVERYBODY'S INTERESTED

Let it be clear. I am demanding the *ability* to opt-out from the government as *an option*. We should all demand this as an option, *even if we have no intention of ever using it*. If we believe in freedom, then it is only right. But asking for the right to have this option is not the same thing as saying that we should want to choose to live this way.

These days, Americans are engaged in what is commonly called the "culture war." We are attempting to transform the world around us to reflect our individual ideals and values. But think about this for a second. The fundamental challenge of democracy, in this or any other country, is that we have hundreds of millions of people who are each quite different from each other and yet are all demanding that the world around them conforms to their own beliefs and values. Naturally, as anyone who thinks about this for a second can see, there is bound to be some amount of tension and conflict in such a situation.

I like to think of myself as a fair-minded person. In this book, I have put some of my political beliefs aside, up until now, because I don't feel that they are particularly relevant to you and

23

I have no desire to attempt to convince anyone to see things my way. You know your values and ideas and I respect you for them. You know who you are and what you want. You know what's best for your life. I respect you and want you to live in a country where you can live according to your ideals. But let's be adults and admit that sometimes your values can conflict with mine. The most important thing to you, for example, might be winning the war in Afghanistan. The most important thing to you might be increasing Defense Industry spending because maybe you work for Lockheed Martin and want your company to do well. Maybe the most important thing to you is increasing the number of cops on the street. Perhaps, for whatever reason, you do not want any of your tax money going to social justice. You may not even want to explain your political beliefs in a rational way. You don't have to.

At the same time, you should try to understand the feelings of others who aren't like you (I'll tell you why in a minute). It was difficult for me to watch my hard-earned tax-money being used for the invasion of Iraq, for the large-scale and ongoing killing of people who did not attack us, when all of the reasons given were lies. During much of the 2000's, I felt like I *wanted out* of that entire system. Then, watching my hard-earned money go to save a bunch of bankers who gambled everything away and deserve to go bankrupt…that also makes me sick. However, to be completely honest, watching my tax-money go to my Grandma taking advantage of Medicare in her old age, watching my tax money go to the unemployment check for my brother who lost his job because his company closed up shop in Wisconsin and relocated to Mexico, watching some of my tax money going to the public education of my nephew…let's just say that I will gladly pay my taxes when it is used in these ways. Why?

I sometimes doubt *my own infallibility*. I often wonder whether things might go south in my life and maybe someday I'll be in need of a little help. I also don't want to walk down the street and deal with a bunch of people starving to death or freezing to death out in the cold because our government chooses not to offer some basic level of assistance. I want to live in a place that is better than that. So I admit it; I don't mind a very minimum safety net if people aren't abusing it on a massive scale. I also believe every child deserves a basic opportunity to succeed in this life...a life that will always be an uphill battle for most of us regardless of how much help we receive.

But so what? Maybe we agree on some things or maybe we don't. The point is, being a citizen in a democracy means that I'll suck it up and deal with some things that *I don't* agree with as long as I feel I am also getting some of the things I *do* agree with. That's the whole point of government! Government isn't only about serving *your own, personal interests*. You shouldn't try to force me to be a part of a government that does only what you think it should do. How ridiculous would it be for you to tell me that I should be happy about taking part in a government that only does things which I am opposed to? Just the same, I can't tell you that you should want to take part in a government in which all Defense spending is cut, in which maybe the right to practice religion in public is not guaranteed, in which maybe the road will never be repaired on the street *where you live*. I don't have the right to do that to you...not at least without offering you the option to opt-out. See, *the least* you should demand is that I am not able to take *your* money solely to carry out *my* agenda (not without *also* making an effort to take care of your agenda). If things do come to that, then I think we should all at least have the option to "leave it". That's why the Total Freedom Act is important.

Let's not pretend that all of America is like you, or that it ever will become so. In return, I won't pretend it is like me or ever will become so. We are free people at heart and we are all a bit (maybe even a lot) different. I am standing right before you and offering evidence that not everyone thinks alike. Even if you do think like me, then I'll gladly go out and find someone who disagrees with both of us only to prove my point.

So we should all be free to make a fundamental decision about whether or not to take part in our government. It is a decision about whether or not we think that the benefits we receive from taking part in our democracy are great enough that we want to continue. If the time comes when we feel that the answer is "no", we should be free to walk away and try something different. To take part in a democracy means to take part in a never-ending quest for *solutions*. How can we expect people to take part in this quest for solutions when they have no fundamental choice to begin with and are *being forced* to take part in it? How can we feel free when we are obviously not free?

Maybe you are a true Libertarian. You believe that the free market will solve all problems. In that case, you should free yourself from government and, purely out of fairness, you should not be benefiting from any of the things that government provides. If you want to stay completely true to your ideals, then you should be able to mail your driver's license (a government-issued permit to drive on government-built roads) along with a statement that you are opting out as a tax-payer under the Total Freedom Act. Just as you wish, you will never be forced to file income tax again. You will forgo any future Social Security benefits. You will forgo any future Medicare / Medicaid benefits. You will resign from any company or organization receiving money from the government (because, obviously, that would be unfairly benefiting from other people's taxes). You will withdraw your children from public schools. Your local government-funded police and fire departments will be notified that they do not need to respond to any incidents concerning you or your property. You will not have access to the courts in case you are wronged by an individual or organization. You will not receive unemployment benefits if you lose your job. You will not be allowed to use the post office. You will not be able to drive on roads that were paid for with other people's taxes. You will have no right to vote. You won't even be able to go to a sports event if the stadium was built with government money. Let me ask though, from one mature adult to another, is this in fact *what you want* when you declare that government is the problem?

You might think the solution, as I'm putting it, is a bit too extreme. But don't you understand? Putting yourself entirely at the mercy of the free market *is* extreme! Total faith in the free market is a radical idea that requires *real-world sacrifice*. Even *this*, what I am proposing, seems unfair to everyone else because you would still be kept safe by the US Military. You would still be benefiting from buying groceries and other goods that are cheap because they were so efficiently transported using the public infrastructure. Your food would still be made less expensive because of government farm subsidies. You would still be benefiting from basic law and order around you (though the police would not protect you, personally). Perhaps you would even, unfairly to others, still be allowed to walk on public side-walks or ride in other people's cars (though of course you will not be allowed to drive your own car on a publically-built road, use city buses, the subway, or any other form of publically-funded transportation). I suppose maybe you could use the airports, though I think most of them are probably paid for by the government as well. Look, if this were *completely fair* to everyone else who is paying taxes, you shouldn't be allowed to even ride in a car or walk on the sidewalk at all! But I'm reasonable and I would be willing to make a few concessions like this just to make this dream possible…this dream of restoring the possibility of complete freedom in America…this dream you have of going back to a time before our government created all of this. I want this for you if this is what you truly want.

If you are, indeed, a Libertarian and choose to opt-out under the Total Freedom Act, then obviously you are the kind of person who believes that the market solves all problems. If there is a need, then the market will deliver a solution to fill it, right? Perhaps there will be enough of you that there will be a new market for flying cars to avoid the problem of not being allowed to drive.

If you are a Libertarian and against government benefits, I'm sure that you don't need to worry about losing your job and needing unemployment. I'm sure you've also saved enough over the years that you won't need Social Security in your old age. Otherwise, quite frankly, it wouldn't make any sense for you to hold the beliefs you do. If you are not independently wealthy, wouldn't it be far too risky to put such beliefs into action? I also sincerely hope you would never have to worry about a long recession or even another Great Depression coming along. And if something tragic like that does happen in your lifetime, I'm sure you'll be able to count on private charity to take care of you, right? This is basically what you believe, right? I respect your beliefs and I hope your theories are, once and for all, proven correct. How sad that we have had to go on arguing all of these ideas in theory when they could be actually proven in reality. It would be pretty exciting to live your dream and have a chance to prove that you are right!

Let's go a bit further. You believe that if the market is left alone, it will provide a better, more prosperous future. You believe in private industry. I'm sure you're not worried that your private employer might discriminate against you if they don't like your political ideas or your religious beliefs. If your boss does fire you because she's a Liberal and is against your ideas, of course you will have no access to the courts to fight this decision. I'm sure you also believe that, if indeed people were given the option to opt-out under the Total Freedom Act, so many people would do this that you would not be alone…that an entirely new economy would spring up that serves you and all of your fellow Libertarians quite well. The market solves all problems, right? Is there not a market of people who want Total Freedom, just as you do? Are there not enough of you to create a market for new products and services that will more efficiently replace the role of government?

It is not my place to question your beliefs or your theories. It is *your dream* to live in a way that is free from government, in a place where the free market solves all of the problems we currently face, where every dollar you earn stays in your pocket and is only used for your benefit. I have no problem with you making the decision to live according to your dreams, according to your ideas, and according to your values. This is what you want and I have no right to insist that you cannot have it. Actually, I sincerely hope all of this becomes possible and all of this works out just as you imagine. That's exactly what I'm arguing for here.

I will only say that, as a necessary part of this Total Freedom Act, when anyone is caught trying to benefit from the government in any way (working in an organization that receives any funding from the government, driving on a government road unlicensed, calling 911, etc.), the penalty is that, first of all, you lose the privilege of your tax-free existence. You will be forced to resume paying taxes immediately or you will face the standard penalties of tax-evasion. Furthermore, before your government benefits will resume, you will also have to back-pay all of the taxes from the years you spent living under the Total Freedom Act. If you cannot afford to do so, you will have to continue paying taxes but receive no benefits. The benefits you willingly gave up will only become available to you again when you are completely up-to-date on back-taxes.

So please be very careful about entering this Total Freedom Act program. If you violate the rules, or if you decide to return to life as a tax-paying citizen, it will cost you what you owe. If, in a time of need you end up looking to the government (which you indicated that you didn't need and stopped contributing to), then you have to do what's fair. Obviously you agree that it's fair…that you cannot spend your entire life not paying-in to Social Security, for example, and then as soon as you are ready to retire and need this benefit switch back to becoming a tax-payer. Of course you *can* go back to becoming a tax-payer at any time, but in doing so you have to pay all of the unpaid taxes from the years you were not paying. Only then will your benefits be restored. If you cannot afford to do so, then it would be entirely unfair for the taxpayers to take care of you…not when you haven't done your part to *help them out* when they needed you. So you have to approach this very important decision with a strong sense of personal responsibility and accountability.

Exercising your option to live under the Total Freedom Act would be a very serious, very real, and very scary decision. Like any such decision in life, there is no going back unless you can pay your way back. Just as the early American settlers knew when they bravely chose to follow their dream of freedom and got on that ship with a one-way ticket, there was no going back unless they could earn enough money in the new land to pay for a return ticket. So it is really quite simple: your back-taxes are your ticket back to the life that taxpayers enjoy.

It is interesting to think about some of the many reasons why people would, indeed, opt-out under the Total Freedom Act. There were moments, in recent history, when I've become so disgusted with the US Government that it felt like to pay taxes to this system is to go against everything I stand for as a human being. Some activists take their beliefs very seriously. Some go on hunger-strikes and some willingly go to prison, so I'm sure there would be some who would, indeed, take the option to live under the Total Freedom Act. Even those who have great faith in government in theory, perhaps even Socialists or Communists, still might choose to opt-out under the Total Freedom Act because they don't believe in the US Government for moral reasons (like their opposition to unjustified wars based on lies). Of course these people should also be free to live according to their values. In doing so, they would be making a powerful statement and I would respect them greatly. I don't think I am that brave.

Do you think we should allow corporations to opt out as well? I don't really see how that makes sense. After all, what is a corporation? Think about it. What do you do when you, as a business-person, want to form a corporation (or a company of any kind)? You go to the government! A business is not, after all, something *separate from* the government! We talk of "public" and "private" as though it is something completely disconnected. But, in fact, a company is an entity *created by the government!* A business organization is also controlled by *laws* created by the government (financial reporting, licensing, trade practices, etc.). Actually, it isn't even intellectually honest to pretend that business is something that is separate from government.

So, while individuals who have opted-out under the Act should be free to conduct business outside of the government's control, companies cannot opt-out from government because they are a *creation of* government. Individuals were created by nature, but businesses are artificial entities created by the government. How would they function, anyway, if not operating under the laws of the land? Perhaps entrepreneurs operating under the Total Freedom Act could still form "unofficial companies" of independent people, but this entity could not be defined in legal terms and it may be difficult to figure out ways to fund and operate it.

Everything a corporation does is defined by the law. Companies rely on the government to enforce contract law, establish accounting standards, and maintain an economic environment in which businesses can thrive. Without government, there would be no standard way for a company to function and no fundamental trust between investors, managers, employees, and customers. For example, if you were unable to establish a legal business entity (which, as I said, requires government involvement), how would a company even determine such basic issues as whose name is attached to the bank account where the money is received or kept? See, the funds that a firm uses to operate are legally owned by the company, not by any of the individuals within the company. So indeed, there can be no functional company or corporation *without* government performing the role of oversight.

The wealthy elite could also choose to opt-out from paying taxes and participating in the US Government. Most of them got rich through business, right? So they probably don't depend much on government, right? Of course, a rich person living under the Total Freedom Act could not own or work for organizations which have government contracts or receive government assistance of any kind (like banks or Wall Street investment firms or, actually, most US corporations who all seem to do some business with the government). An individual living under the protection of the Total Freedom Act shouldn't even be able to hold the stocks of these companies (at least a portion of the stock price is based on government contracts and government assistance, right?). They shouldn't be allowed to contribute money to political causes either, as it wouldn't be allowed to take part in politics when you have opted-out under the Total Freedom Act. They probably would have no reason to contribute money anyway, not when they aren't able to receive contracts or any kind of favors or indirect kick-backs *from* government. That's why they make these contributions to candidates today, right?

Do you think that the wealthy elites understand how much they benefit from government? I'll bet my money that they do. Why do you think they contribute so much money, willingly, to political causes (even as they do everything in their power to avoid paying taxes)? As I have said, they do it because, when they are able to buy off politicians, they get our tax money funneled straight to them through contracts, subsidies, and bailouts. So we might be surprised to find out that the rich *would not* opt-out under the Act. I'm sure they like things fine just the way they are. They don't want a free-market…not exactly. They mostly just want *their status quo* protected as they talk about the free market. Lately, the government is doing a pretty damn good job to serving upper-class.

Other individuals might choose, as I have done, to look for a better life elsewhere. We certainly shouldn't have to answer to the US Government at all (as we currently do). We should be free to file ourselves under the Total Freedom Act as well. If we want to come back and re-enter civic life in the US, we either have to pay any owed taxes or prove that we are up-to-date on any taxes owed from the income earned wherever else we have lived. Today, we can still vote while we are abroad, but I would even be willing to give up that right while I'm away. It doesn't seem fair that I have a say in elections but don't have to suffer the consequence of the results on a daily basis. But we should certainly not be forced to file anything having to do with taxes while we are living abroad.

There are certainly other reasons, which I'm probably overlooking, that people might choose to opt-out under the Total Freedom Act. Once again, I'm not arguing that I, personally, would choose to opt-out if I were living in the US. In complete honesty, I would probably come to the personal conclusion that, while I'm passionately opposed to probably 90% of what the US Government has been doing in recent years, I still see *enough of a benefit* just in terms of the services I've mentioned that I would continue paying taxes. I'm quite sure, actually, that the vast majority of Americans would come to this same conclusion. So I'm certainly not suggesting that this should be a widely-used program. Very few are brave enough to follow their ideals to the extent that they are willing to pay a very real price in their real lives. Most of us would choose to live in the state of imperfection, just as we do today. Most of us, if we are being completely honest, would choose some degree of safety and comfort even if it does make us a bit hypocritical to do so. But all of us would like to have the option.

Everyone should be afforded this opportunity...this chance to live according to their dreams and ideals if they so choose. For so many brave, patriotic Americans, that means returning to a kind of freedom only known by those original settlers. These brave Americans of today don't want to live in some foreign land. They don't want a non-stop culture war that seemingly cannot be won. Why force them to enter the political realm they so obviously detest, to operate within government when they inherently do not believe in government? All they want is to be free from government! What they are saying (if we are to believe them at their word), is that they just want to live self-sufficiently and on their own terms. They want the government out of their lives. They simply want America to truly become the land of the free again…the place where certain things are possible which are not possible anywhere else. Is this really too much to ask?

6 MY PARTY IS IN POWER AND THE PACKERS WON!

Let's take a step back from discussing this Total Freedom Act. Maybe I'm getting a bit ahead of myself. Maybe it is sounding a bit too crazy to you...imagining a life without government. So let's assume (as I have argued) that the vast majority of Americans would not use the Total Freedom Act. So let's look at the democracy we *actually do have*. Let's discuss the very *idea of* American Democracy.

Maybe you believe in the process. Maybe you think I was being too harsh or cynical in the "To the Ruling Elite" chapter. After all, it is purely American to have complete faith in democracy. These are our elected officials, right? They are accountable to us, right? America is the shining example of democracy, right? So naturally those of us who take part in American politics (either as a voter, campaigner, activist, protester, candidate, or politician) are proudly taking part in what we believe is a meaningful endeavor that will surely have an impact. Why else are we doing it? Liberal, Conservative, Independent, Tea Party, Libertarian, Green, Anarchist...we should all be able to agree that it is completely possible to achieve our goals through the political process.

I really want to believe in this. But if I'm being completely honest, it does bother me a bit that, throughout our history, both Democrats and Republicans constantly seem to make generic promises that sound good pre-election and then get into office only to ignore or explain away everything they had just promised. Maybe we've occasionally seen them deviate from this course only to stumble around in their own stupidity or naivety, but soon enough the "party-machine" seems to come along in order to get them back in line.

I don't mean to be cynical, because *theoretically* I know how we can solve our problems through Washington's institutions. But sometimes it does seem like game is rigged and that we, personally, have almost no impact as citizens. Doesn't it sometimes seem like just that these days – a game? I've been paying close attention for a least a decade or two and of course I've noticed that the two parties do, in fact, look and sound very different from each other. But then when you look at the results…the actual policy decisions…the system just seems to hum along, uninterrupted, whoever is in power. That might be all well-and-good, but the problem is that it seems to be not so much "humming" anymore but spinning out of control and crashing.

Indeed, we often say that politics is a game, or theater, or a show. I've been thinking lately that American politics *is* like a sport. This is, without a doubt, the best analogy. When I think about sports, I remember my childhood in central Wisconsin, home of the Green Bay Packers. In this part of the world, when the Packers win a game on Sunday, everything is right with the world. When they lose, we are barely able to face Monday. As I watch elections sway one way or the other, I've noticed this same element in politics as well. Regardless of whether Democrats or Republicans are in power, half of the country seems to feel that everything is great and the other half feels like the world is upside down for a few years. In fairness, make that 25% and 25% of the country, because the other half of the country doesn't even care to vote.

I remember what it is like at a Packer game. I've only been to one Packer game as a young child, by the way, because it is really hard to get tickets. But from far back in the cheap seats on that cold afternoon, I remember that even my Dad's loudest shouts had no real impact on our team's performance. I don't even remember who won that game, to be honest, just that they played the Chicago Bears. I guess, over the long-term, whether or not our favorite team wins or loses in sports, our lives are not actually changed. Maybe our mood shifts a bit when our favorite team wins, but we have to admit that nothing really changes in our lives other than the fact that we just paid a lot of money for the thrilling experience of going to the game.

What does this have to do with politics? I *hope*, and I certainly want to believe, that my experience as a Packer fan is not a direct analogy for US politics. Certainly, we must believe that our lives are directly affected when one party wins or the other, right? I'm sure you've noticed meaningful change in your life when the right party is in power, right?

Let's think about the Bush years, for example. All that military spending kept us safe, aside from the horrible tragedy of 9/11 of course. Yet if I'm being completely honest, I wasn't too worried about Al Qaida hitting my neighborhood because I didn't see anything around that they'd care about in my neighborhood. I actually wasn't so scared of Al Qaida at all after the initial shock of 9/11 wore off. I hope you don't find that to be offensive for any reason, I just want to be honest about my personal feelings (though I certainly respect yours if they are different). But as I was saying, maybe if you live in a symbolically-important area, then maybe you felt much safer because of the War on Terror.

Bush also overthrew Saddam and put him to death. I guess I should have been bothered that the power-hungry dictator was still in charge in Iraq. But to be completely honest, it didn't bother me that much or affect my real life because there are a lot of brutal dictators around the world and I try not to lose too much sleep over it. But I don't want to say that you shouldn't care a lot about this because perhaps this did have a direct effect on your real life somehow.

At least, during the Bush presidency, there were no blow-jobs in the Oval Office that we know of. That was really bothering me in the late 1990's. Well, the act itself wouldn't have bothered me too much I guess. What was really bothering me was hearing all about every embarrassing detail in the media for what seemed like years and years. Still, other than having to deal with what I see when watching TV (this is starting to sound a lot like a Packer game), I'm still having a hard time figuring out how any of these events in American politics affected my *real* life.

There must surely have been ways that Bush changed our real lives. I know he was talking about overturning Roe v. Wade, though he didn't quite pull that one off. Well, when I think about that a bit longer, maybe it doesn't really bother me *that much* that people who I don't even know sometimes decide to have an abortion as a response to life circumstances that don't involve me and that I don't exactly understand. I mean, I would never want my wife or daughter to do such a thing, but then again I really don't think *they would*. But I can understand if this is something you worry about. Besides, this change didn't actually happen anyway. Sorry to bring it up.

Didn't the Bush wars make gas cheaper? It would make sense, since practically our entire military was over there occupying oil-rich Iraq. I did wonder though, quietly to myself at the time, how much of my tax money went to pay for that enormous effort. I mean, when you factor all of that into what we actually end up paying for fuel, was gas really any cheaper at all? I don't think so. Then again, didn't gas prices get really high by the end of his presidency anyway? So we can forget that argument. I did hear something about the Oil companies and the commodities traders doing really well during that time though, so if you work for them or have family who does I can certainly understand how the Bush Administration has had a real and positive impact on your real life. If I'm being completely honest, when I think of the Bush years, I'm sorry to say that I can't remember anything that the government did to change my *real* life for the better in any real way. I don't want to over-simplify like that. I'm sure I'm overlooking something. Maybe you could point it out and, in that case, I stand corrected. But off the top of my head I really can't think of it.

That's not to say that government doesn't concern me or give me a lot to worry about. What I worry most about when it comes to our government is the enormous and constantly growing deficit. I do worry that, if these guys can't get themselves under control, they will completely wreck the economy. They will get us so far into debt that, when it eventually becomes clear that they can't pay back creditors, they will destroy the dollar and we will suddenly be asked to pay enormous taxes just to pay for all of their previous wasteful spending. That could have a scary and very real impact on our lives someday. Republicans are always promising that they will reverse this trend of ever-increasing spending and an ever-increasing debt. Yet it still just continues to grow, sometimes even at a faster pace, even when they are in power. But since *they say* that they are the party of less government and less spending, I guess we are supposed to have no doubt that they are being honest about this and intend to do just that in the future. Right?

Now don't even get me started on the Democrats. They don't seem to even understand the benefits of business and free market economics. Instead, they get in there and enact so many socialist policies that it's truly amazing our economy is still running at all. Just look at Obamacare. I think that at some point in the future there were going to be some changes that I think were going to change something about some people's health insurance policies if Republicans don't end up reversing them or something (but I can't exactly remember what those changes really are). I did hear that we will be required to buy health insurance. That's right, we will be *required* by government force to take our hard-earned money and give it to insurance companies, who keep raising our premiums and gouging us further each year! That's not right. Even though this is really messed up, I don't know how bothered I am about this healthcare bill in contrast to everything else going on. But I do know that the cost of healthcare is ridiculous (and going up so fast that I don't know how anybody can keep up). I just think people ought to be able to go to the doctor when they are sick and not face the threat of going bankrupt as a result. Sometimes it seems like the problem is not so much government-run healthcare (which of course we still don't have), but the greedy insurance companies, hospitals, and ambulances charging such ridiculous prices when we are guilty only of becoming sick, injured, and therefore defenseless. I don't actually know if blaming the whole problem on some kind of socialist takeover makes all that much sense. But the problems with our healthcare system could easily fill this book from cover-to-cover, so I'll put that problem aside for now.

I can tell you I was really bothered, though, by all the money that went to bailing out the investment banks, bailing out General Motors, etc. As I said, I believe in Capitalism, and in basic free-market economics. So, if we're going to call this system "capitalist", then it would seem that when a company runs itself into bankruptcy…then it should fail. I'd like to believe that Republicans would never have done such a thing. But then again, they did approve the first bank bailout just before Obama was elected. I guess they had no choice, though, because the bankers were saying that the economy was on the verge of collapse. But either way, I still can't really tell whether this had any impact on our real lives. I don't work on Wall Street or for General Motors. So I wouldn't have minded seeing those bastards go out of business (especially those criminal, elitist little pricks on Wall Street). But maybe you directly benefited from

Wall Street or work for General Motors. In that case, I can certainly see where this bailout affected your life directly and I'm sorry if what I said sounded selfish or offensive to you.

Come to think of it, I don't actually see a lot of difference between the reality of life under the Bush Administration and life under the Obama Administration. We just want government out of our lives, right? We want all those programs which don't make sense to be cut, right? We want our taxes cut, right? We want to believe that if we can get the right people into power, they will make this happen. They will cut all the waste, close departments, and cut wasteful spending. If we can just get the right people elected I know that this change is coming! We *can* find virtuous politicians who don't want only to boost their own power, who don't want only to funnel our tax money into organizations they are connected to, who will not act on a quid-pro-quo basis, who will put their personal ambitions aside and think about the good of the people for once. God, lately this is getting harder and harder to believe.

But let's try some positive thinking. Surely we can find enough of these incorruptible politicians to form a majority and actually make it happen, right? And they will find a way to raise all the money they need to advertise, navigate all the corrupt games in Washington, and make real change happen from within a system that seems more and more corrupt by the day. Sure, it's possible. It's just that, over these past two hundred years or so, we've seen only the opposite: bigger government, more corruption, less freedom, more interference, more power concentration and, at least in recent decades, less improvement in the lives of regular people.

American Democracy is the best in the world and this is exactly what the people are fighting for, right? It just takes a while, right? We have to stay at it and not become cynical. We cannot give-in to the belief that it is all just a game to distract us for a few moments while they continue screwing us over each day, each week, and each month with no apparent end in sight. Right?

The reality is that I can't remember a damn thing that came out of Washington in my lifetime that has really changed anything about my actual life for the better. Maybe you can. In that case, I guess I'm not seeing something. Maybe I'm biased or maybe I just have bad luck.

7 A PLAN TO GET REELECTED

So let's go back to the question of government in our lives and the idea of the Total Freedom Act. Those in government; whether Democrat, Republican, Tea Party, Independent, Green or anyone else, should have nothing at all to fear about the Total Freedom Act. Any student of political science and any observer of human nature should know that people cannot be effectively governed without consent. Only 50% of the country votes every few years and, in total, roughly 25% - 30% of the country actually ends up making the final decision to elect one party or the other. This, alone, doesn't mean that you have a mandate. This doesn't even make the government legitimate. You cannot govern without a mandate and you can't get a mandate unless you first have consent to govern.

Perhaps this explains why the Great American Experiment went so stunningly well in the early years. Remember, people actually *opted-in* to becoming Americans. That's because most of them were not born here or, if they were, then at some point in the very recent past their parents or grandparents opted-in by making the long journey to this great country. But, after many generations, the population is now far removed from that decision. The slow but steady decay we are seeing today might have something to do with the fading, now basically non-existent memory of that moment when each and every American said "yes" to taking part in America. Whether saying "yes" means taking part in government or being free from it, we can now experience that moment again! We can even do it *this year*! Why not?

But I should also warn you, those of you already in office, that if you are kind enough to give us this freedom, you can no longer continue to run for reelection with the message of "getting Washington out of our lives" – not unless you are fighting for the Total Freedom Act. But if you are not a proponent of this idea, you can no longer run on Ronald Reagan's message of small government or, indeed, getting rid of government. The words are nice, but the action is better. And how shameful it would be, now that you've heard this simple and realistic idea I have proposed, to continue using this message to gain support when you know, full-well, that you could very easily deliver exactly as you promised. Maybe you or your supporters haven't previously thought of this as a real option, the idea of this Total Freedom Act, but now you understand that this *is* a good idea and is a very real answer to our modern-day ideological culture war. So instead of running your next election on yet another empty promise, you can run on the idea that you have *finally fulfilled this promise* in the most *real way* imaginable. I'm offering you the answer right here, in this short book. You, as a true patriot, can soon say that you have delivered the chance at total freedom to every American! You can say that you, personally, have restored America as that place of *true freedom*! Do it before your opponent does!

I'm convinced that you guys can lead the charge and make this happen without causing any real havoc or interruption to the system at all. Even after this bill passes, very few people would want to opt-out of the government you are part of, would they? Instead, what you'd be left with is a population that wants to be part of the solution, not part of the problem. When you pass this legislation, they will not feel demoralized and in despair, as so many of them do today. They will finally feel *respected* by you. They will finally be treated, by Uncle Sam, as the adults that they are.

It seems to me that, once this idea has been shared far and wide, any politician who would continue to run on the small-government message…that there's nothing we can do to get government out of our lives other than electing yet another politician making the same generic promises we've already heard for decades…would be completely disingenuous. Anybody running on a message of small government *should be asked* about their support for the Total Freedom Act. Anybody who truly believes in these principles should support it. So, unfortunately for you, now that this idea has been put forth, you might have to change your approach a bit. I know, the other approach was working quite well to get you elected, but the message is getting kind of stale and it is certainly time to find a new bag of tricks. Sorry about that. I'm not saying you've been disingenuous all these years. Maybe you just didn't think of this. But either way, you do have to change your tune now. I'm sure that you have plenty of talented strategists who will come up with something. Then again, you may not need much help in this area because you will be so popular after enacting this historic legislation that you will get yourself reelected by a landslide.

As we move forward, assuming this idea has been spread, the only reason I can see for *not* wanting to give people this true and genuine chance at freedom is that you want to continue winning elections by making disingenuous promises which you have no intention to keep. What else can we conclude, after watching the way you guys have operated for all these years? And now, after hearing about this idea, what are we to think if you were to ignore it?

At this moment, as a politician, you are at an interesting cross-road. We followed you as you walked us here, now it is time for you to lead us all the way to the destination you've been telling us about. Give the people what you have been promising: give them the chance to get the government off their backs and let them experience the wonders of the free market. Once again, a person who has opted-out will also not be a burden to the government. As far as you're concerned, it is as though he or she were never born at all. Better yet, the remaining voters will finally be interested in real solutions. New ideas will enter the political arena and be accepted by the population because everybody taking part will actually have chosen to take part in the system that governs them.

Oh, and whatever you do with this idea, I'm going to ask one thing: do not dare attempt to use moral arguments against it. Do not attempt to tell us that you cannot allow people to opt-out as tax-payers and forgo government services because you care about them, because we have a duty to make sure innocent kids aren't punished due to the decisions of their parents. *Don't you dare* make this into a moral argument! Why not?

First of all, you have no right to lecture these people. They are Americans. They were born with certain inalienable rights and one of them is the right to freedom. Don't you dare pretend that you care anything about morality here. Where is the morality in being part of a system that sends kids off to die in a war based on lies? Where is the morality in not providing every child (no, actually every person) with guaranteed access to healthcare? In case you haven't noticed, you *are not* part of a government that is grounded in morality. Whether Democrat or Republican, *do not pretend* that yours is a government that represents morality at all or I might stop by just to throw up on a staffer's shoes at your next fundraiser.

America is the only country where this idea makes sense. *Precisely because* we fall short so badly in terms of social justice and morality in our government and in our economy, this chance at total freedom is a unique opportunity. Only after you've taken some very real steps toward making this a moral country where we take care of each other and respect each other, then I'll shut up about this Total Freedom Act. But as things are, you simply have no moral ground to stand on. People are not being taken care of! But if you are truly concerned, perhaps we can make some moral considerations like trying to make sure that children are still protected to some extent under the law of the land (regardless of the choices their parents make). I'm sure these questions will be worked out as you begin drafting the legislation. Maybe, while you're at it, you can make sure that every single child has healthcare (just like old people do). I'll even help you with the verbiage. It takes just one sentence: "All children under the age of 18 are now covered by Medicare." Simple.

You can also stop looking down on people and pretending that they don't know what is in their own best interests. More likely, they see you and what you are up to quite clearly, indeed. Having us trapped is not the same thing as having us fooled. Please just give us our right to freedom and then do everything you can to throw us a tasty enough bone every now and then so that we don't actually exercise it. But, either way, you do not have the right to claim control over our lives on moral grounds just because you happen to sit in some luxurious stone building in Washington, D.C. Nope, you have to back it up with something. As things stand today, I'm not seeing it.

Indeed, it is only our consent which gives you any right over our lives. I don't care how smart you are, how rich you are, how powerful you are, or how many influential people you know. Even if you are not on our side and care nothing about us, you have to at least start respecting us as human beings. If nothing else, shut up about your anti-government rhetoric unless you really mean it. Pay up or shut up.

8 TO THE DISINGENUOUS

In writing this book, I have attempted to give every American the benefit of the doubt. I want to believe that we are all fighting for what we truly believe is right. I want to believe that every idea I hear in this sickening culture war is at least an *honest* idea presented in a way that is not disingenuous. We are all just trying to change the world to make it the kind of place we would like to live in, right?

But I can't help thinking that there are people out there who are willing to use any kind of political argument only to make us believe one thing while they are getting away with another. So I think it would be wise for the otherwise innocent and well-meaning among us to be careful, to look out for ourselves a bit. I'm just saying…I know you exist. Next time I see you on TV with your "government is the problem" message, next time I hear you saying that you want to cut spending on social programs, that you don't believe in social justice, that you want to cut programs that don't work, I only hope, for your sake, that at some point you get *very specific*. I don't want to hear anything as vague as "eliminating wasteful spending". Either that or I would suggest booking lots and lots of interviews quickly because your window of opportunity is closing. People are going to start catching on. You might eventually have to look for a new job, like so many other Americans do these days.

I know there are a lot of you out there making lots of money and getting lots of exposure with this anti-government message. I can't keep track of all of you, but most likely you are working for someone with a lot of power who is trying to carry out some sort of hidden agenda (more about that agenda in a moment). Maybe you're one of the honest few who believe your own anti-government, libertarian message for pure reasons. I'll take you on your word if you say so, but unfortunately there are a lot people out there who are spreading the anti-government message for all the wrong reasons. Come to think of it, the only way to know which side you are on is to *ask you about your support for the Total Freedom Act*. I hope this question starts to come up during your appearances. Maybe it already has, and that's why you're reading this book.

Let me explain this in a very simple way. If you *do not* support the Total Freedom Act, if you talk about eliminating government in our lives and yet still want us to pay taxes into government, I can only conclude that you just want your hands on our money. I get it. These days your employers, sponsors, and handlers are quite satisfied because they are watching the vast majority of our tax money end up right in the hands of private industry. They argue that private business works better than government and, using that reasoning, turn our tax money over to private companies to run nearly every function that the government should be doing. Private security companies like Xe Services LLC (formerly Blackwater) are doing what the US Military should be doing in Iraq and Afghanistan. Private prison facilities like Correctional Services Corporation are imprisoning Americans for a profit and then making them work while in prison so they can earn even more profit. Private health insurance companies like Blue Cross Blue Shield are making a profit by performing a function that government arguably should be doing. You even want charter schools and for-profit universities to make a profit doing what public schools and state universities should be doing. I'm just getting started. The government also hands over our tax money, in the form of farm subsidies, to enormous corporations like Monsanto (there aren't many small farmers anymore). The examples of corporate hand-outs are endless, and all of it is justified with the logic that "government is bad". The simple problem here is that a very large portion of my tax money goes directly to corporations (and then right to rich executives as bonuses and to investors as profit). That doesn't seem right…not when the middle class is sliding into poverty.

You talk a good game about the free market, but where is the free market in this exactly? If you actually understood the free market, you'd know that it has to do with how capitalists (not tax-payers) *willingly* invest money into businesses. Companies then deliver a product or service to the market and consumers (not taxpayers) buy it if they want it. I don't remember Adam Smith talking about how the government was supposed to take our money through taxes and give it directly to businesses. That has nothing to do with the free market and to argue that it does is a complete distortion.

If this is your game, I suppose it does bother you when a portion of our tax money does, indeed, continue to go into programs that only end up benefiting the people directly (with no profit to you). Any dollar that goes into Welfare, Unemployment, Social Security, Medicare, or Public Education is a dollar that can't be funneled to your people. I get your game. You use some good ideas (free market economic theory) to try to convince me to let you get your hands on my tax money. I do admire your effort, but unfortunately for you I see through it.

I see how you guys finance political campaigns in return for favors. I see how you guys pay expensive lobbyists to keep politicians under control when they are in office. Naturally, you have to make sure the government is responsive to your contributions just as you attempt to keep us, the taxpayer, in line with your dishonest and disingenuous arguments. How else would you be able to swindle us out of our money on such a massive scale? But this is a question you will not be able to keep dodging forever. If you truly support freedom, as you say you do, if you truly believe that government is bad, if you *truly believe in the free market*, then you will support the Total Freedom Act. And you know what? Tell your boss or your sponsor or whoever the hell gave you your script that, *if they want my money, they will have to earn it in the marketplace by delivering a product or service that I actually want.* I hope your business skills are as good as your skills as propagandist. I want you to succeed, so I'll give you a tip: I hear flying cars will be hot next year.

9 ENDING GOVERNMENT THROUGH GOVERNMENT

The Total Freedom Act is, quite simply, the right idea at the right time. It is a realistic plan to restore true freedom in America. It is also just about the only way I can think of to actually have an honest conversation about the idea of getting the government off our backs for those who want just that. It is fair, presumably not a huge hit to the tax base (as I doubt many of even the loudest proponents would take the leap into this program if given the chance), and it is entirely realistic. If you have a better idea, then I'm all ears. Thank you for the opportunity to present mine.

For at least three decades now, America has been stuck in this never-ending cycle of arguing for smaller government, shouting about the evils of government, and touting the virtues of the free market. Yet all we've seen each year (almost without exception) is a government that gets bigger and bigger, intrudes further and further into our lives, becomes more and more corrupt, and funnels more and more of our tax money into big business. Enough is enough! The Total Freedom Act is a simple idea that can put an end to all of this. Now can we finally move forward?

Just to be completely clear, I'm not arguing any of this on a theoretical basis. Remember, I'm only interested in discussing *reality*. I don't mean to suggest that this idea for the Total Freedom Act is something that should "enter the public discourse" in order to "make us think long and hard about the role of government in our lives". God no. I mean, quite simply, that someone should deliver this book to President Obama tomorrow, and in his haste to reach out and make nice with the other side of the isle, he should tell the American people that he plans to rush right down to the Republican-led House of Representatives and ask them to enact this immediately so that he can sign it. At the same time, I mean that the House should be working through the night to draw up this legislation so that it can be put on the President's desk by the end of the week. They should be doing this so that they can take credit for this great idea before the President does!

Now, right after that happens, I'm sure Washington and the cable news programs and all of the blogosphere can go on humming along as it usually does. Those who want to opt-out under the Total Freedom Act can finally tune-out and go on to live their government-free lives in the real world. Those of us who remain as tax-payers can start to have a conversation about some of the things that matter in the real world. We can finally get unstuck from this never-ending train of thought that always ends with the conclusion that government is the enemy. We can start to consider what *we do* want our government to do. More specifically, we can think about what kinds of things the government *has to do* so that we don't reach the point of wanting to opt-out from it.

The successful passage of the Total Freedom Act is just the beginning. I've already described what it is and what it would mean in the lives of real people. I think I've also explained that those who choose to remain as tax-payers and as participants in the US Government would become part of the solution and start seeing things more clearly (but maybe the government can form a committee to do research on this idea just to confirm my hunch…kidding). When we have eliminated today's false and misleading notion of *ending government through government*, we can finally begin looking for other kinds of solutions that might actually make government *work*. We can finally start to end this downward spiral, this long losing season in the game of American politics.

Yet today, as things are, *so many Americans* believe that government isn't just *a* problem, it is *the* problem. This infers that there are *no other problems*, right? I have to admit that I don't think this is entirely true. I do feel oppressed at times in my life. I do feel sometimes that my human dignity is not respected. In truth, the source of this disrespect, this lack of dignity, isn't always the government. I remember applying for jobs in the private sector and being forced to urinate in a cup. I remember working in a window factory back in college (a factory that is now out of business because the jobs were shipped overseas) where showing up five minutes late could get you fired. In the corporate office environment, visiting the wrong website or sending the wrong message on your work computer can also get you fired. They can spy on you all they want and you have nothing to say about it as long as you still want a paycheck. It doesn't feel right. It is a really paranoid way to live. I actually feel dirty and violated *by the private sector*, in these cases, not by government.

Restaurant or customer service workers also know that if they aren't polite enough to customers, if they don't smile the right way, if they don't stay cool even if being disrespected or completely berated by a rude customer, that they can lose their jobs. It feels like nothing other than oppression when we are forced to smile and say the same line 500 times a day (even on a really bad day where you might have broken up with your boyfriend or something) just so that you don't face losing your source of income. I don't mind if my waiter or waitress is a real human. I certainly don't want a fake, smiling robot. Why do we always have to pretend?

Miners, construction workers, and electric company repair people have to risk their safety or even their lives to do what they are told to do at work. My good friend lost his father, who was an electric company employee, due to a terrible accident at work. We have to put up with these risks, we are told, because someone is waiting in line right behind us to take our job if we don't want it. That's the free market at work, right? Tragically, the free market didn't work so well for my friend's father.

If we are to be intellectually honest about the situation, I think we have to consider that, through strong Unions and Governments, people in advanced countries have improved conditions greatly over the years. Long ago, before most of us were born, our parents, grandparents, and great-grandparents achieved some important victories that improved workplace conditions substantially. These brave, idealistic Progressives fought for and earned the 40-hour work week, vacation time, and holidays off. Civil Rights legislation even curbed unfair discrimination in society and in the workplace. These are things that the market, alone, wasn't prepared to offer us. These are things that people had to fight for in other ways. The government ended up being a strong ally in this fight.

I actually believe that none of these points go against the fundamental idea of free-market theory (though some would have us believe differently). Think about it. You could easily say that there is a sort of "demand for" or a "market for" strong governments and even unions. Why else did people fight for them if there wasn't a market demand for them? Perhaps people have a need to live with some minimum level of dignity and, out of this demand, there is a *market incentive* for us to work together and fight together for our own interests. Indeed, I guess we have a *demand for* human dignity that goes back way before our demand for the flat-screen TV! And in developed "human-dignity markets"—that is, in every advanced democracy in the world (perhaps other than the US) – people have come to a consensus on the idea that Government is a part of the *solution*. A strong and functioning government is seen as the primary way that people can fight against the exploitation and dehumanization that we otherwise experience if left to the free market alone.

It is true that market forces have fostered the kind of innovation that has improved our quality of life as consumers, but the free market has also led to harsher realities like children laboring in sweatshops. In countries around the world, so many of the people who find themselves living under corrupt, authoritarian governments are working in terrible conditions and for very little pay. Young children come from poor villages and, with only the modest hope of perhaps feeding the family, they work ridiculously long hours in inhuman conditions. We all know about this because they make most of the stuff we enjoy as consumers. Some people argue that the market will fix this problem, that wages will go up in these places as local skills increase or as demand for labor goes up. But it seems to me that there are more people around the world willing to work hard than there are available jobs. And even after wages do go up in one place, companies will only move manufacturing to somewhere else where the profit margin is higher. Maybe it is just a coincidence that wages are higher, that the standard of living is better, and that human dignity is higher in markets with a tradition of strong pro-worker, pro-people movements (Europe, Canada, and the US historically). Or maybe I'm imagining all of it and it is just a coincidence that somehow the market just tends to work better in these countries?

There is still another side to this story. I guess if I were a wealthy business owner looking for cheap labor so that I could make a larger profit, then I would argue that things "work better" in countries with corrupt governments and terrible labor conditions. So if you earn your living as an investor or as a business owner and, indeed, you want to have operations in China or Mexico or India or wherever, then I can see why you *would not* support a strong government that fights for the well-being of the common person. But if you have a job, then I'd be surprised if you *do not* support a strong government that will fight hard for you.

Sometimes I even wonder whether we truly have a government at all, even today. Have you ever heard the argument that, essentially, corporations own the government and that government is only an arm of corporate power? I can see where some people might get this idea. First of all, so much of the funding for political campaigns comes from corporations. This being the case, who do you think our politicians are serving in their policy-making? Can we be sure, for example, that they cannot be persuaded to take us to war just to please weapons manufacturers and security companies? Wouldn't it be a damn good plan for them to funnel our tax money to themselves while, at the same time, using brute force to obtain access to and ownership of huge oil reserves in Iraq? I can't make a bullet-proof argument that most of the recent wars were done in the interest of resources and corporate profit, but it is at least worth considering as an explanation for what would otherwise appear to be very foolish decision-making. This is exactly what the rest of the world thinks that the US is up to, so I think it is at least worth considering.

Then, when you look at the big bank bailouts, you wonder who we should be angry at. Are we supposed to believe that the government was only acting foolishly when they offered billions of dollars to the banks, or is there something else to it? I find myself feeling most angry at the reckless bankers for messing everything up and then threatening to crash the economy if they would not be able to get their hands on our tax money to fund their bailout. Why would the US Government go along with such a plan? Are they acting out of their own free (political) will or are they simply serving the corporations who put them there? Exactly how many Goldman Sachs people are actually at the highest levels of our government, anyway? See what I'm saying? I mean, most people don't even know this, but the Federal Reserve is not the government. The Federal Reserve, which is responsible for printing and managing our money supply, is owned and operated by the largest banks. Rich bankers print paper and the rest of us are meant to covet that paper more than anything else in life. We all know that money is the mechanism that pretty much controls everything. So when the private banks have this much power over the economy, are we supposed to believe that the government actually had any power to say *no* to the bailout...to let the troubled banks go bankrupt? Does our government actually have *any* power anymore? Is the US a democracy at all, or are we just playing the sport of democracy? This is actually an important question.

What about the oil spill in the Gulf? That was clearly done by a private company. Tell me, would the free market clean that up or does it take a strong government with plenty of resources? What about the loss of jobs in our economy? The government is only at fault because it caved to the pressure of big business when all those free-trade agreements were negotiated in the 1990s. This made it possible for companies to hire cheap labor in other countries instead of more expensive labor (i.e. jobs you could have) in the United States. Who should we be angry at here, the government for interfering in our lives or private companies for using our government to undermine our lifestyle only to create larger profits for themselves?

Who exactly is the enemy, anyway? Is government good and business bad? Is business bad and government good? Are business and government one-and-the-same? See, if we are going to believe that there is some large, powerful force that is working against us in modern-day America, you have to choose your answer.

10 SIMPLE MULTIPLE CHOICE

In America today (not in abstract theory, but in reality), which of the three following options are true? It is simple multiple-choice:

a) Government is good and business is bad
b) Government is bad and business is good
c) Government and business are one-and-the-same

I'm not asking you to answer what you *want* to be true or what you *think* could someday be true. The time for wishful thinking has passed. That is so 1990's. I'm asking you to think about reality as you see it today. Can you think of another possibility other than these three options? I can't. So go ahead, make your selection. The answer to this multiple-choice question is the start of understanding what kind of political movement you will probably find yourself believing in.

If you believe that, in America today, option "a" (government is good and business is bad) is most true, then you must really disagree with most of what I said in this book (my cynical attitude about the US Government). You must think that democracy is working quite well because, after all, Obama is President. You must believe that government is, indeed, serving the interests of the people – that government is something separate from business. Is this really the case though? Perhaps this *might have been true* in the past, in Roosevelt's time for example. I suppose it is always true *to some extent*, but today there doesn't seem to be much truth to it. The only thing the government seems to be doing for the people is maintaining *the few* social programs left, minimal workers rights, and all the other stuff that Libertarians, Tea Party people, and Republicans want to eliminate.

If you selected "b" (that government is bad and business is good), then you also believe that, in the US today, business and government are somehow at-odds and are operating independently. You believe that, without government, businesses would somehow be able to operate differently from how they do…even differently from how *they seem to want to*. You believe that business would better serve you, not better exploit you, if government would just get out of the way. I don't quite understand the logic that business would treat me any better, as an employee for example, if it wasn't for the government trying to protect my rights. Actually I don't get that *at all*. Do you really think the free market would eliminate abusive jobs? I don't. Maybe I'm missing something. If you believe this, though, then you probably want all the programs eliminated that the people who selected option "a" value.

If we do not believe that government can do good, then what we are inevitably left with is a government that does only evil. If you end *good* (well-meaning) social programs like Medicare, social justice programs, environmental programs, Social Security, Unemployment Insurance, libraries, parks, Public Education, etc., then what you are essentially left with is a government that takes money from you through taxes and gives it to private industry. I can't see why you'd want your hard-earned money taken by the government and then given directly to business so they can extract a profit. That would be silly. If I did agree with option "b", then I would consider opting out from taxes altogether and I'd be a strong proponent of the Total Freedom Act. Let's eliminate all government and let the corporations make their own money instead of stealing it from us!

If you mostly identified with option "c", you think that business and government in America today is pretty much the same thing. You think that pretty much everything government does is ultimately to serve the interests of business. You probably don't believe this is *right*, just that this is the way it is. You could say that government is something like the Human Resources department of Corporate America. Just like a Human Resources department, you could say that the government's focus is only to deal with those messy but unavoidable "human issues" while making us believe in the mission of the company.

If you believe in option "c", you probably don't believe that fundamental change can come through elections. You think that the Democrats and Republicans are pretty much the same in that they serve the wealthy elite while ignoring the people. You think this should be different. You probably voted for people like Ralph Nader because you think that government should be a strong, beneficial force that fights to improve the lives of "We the People", does what's right, protects the environment, etc. You want your tax money to stop being handed over to big business. In other words, you want to end corporate welfare. Instead, you want government spending focused on programs that benefit real people, that improve the quality of our real lives, and that make the country a better, more comfortable place to live in.

As for the Republicans and Democrats, over the past several decades, the reality of choosing one or the other is that they are only marginally different. This, in itself, wouldn't be a problem. The problem is that everything only continues to worsen. In other words, the company called America is failing and it doesn't really seem to matter *who* is in charge of "Human Resources".

Even as we all watch and feel this downward spiral, most of us continue to spend our political energies fighting for one party or the other. The proverbial pendulum keeps on swinging back and forth. The problem is that the basic course we are on never seems to change.

Nothing will ever change as long as we remain in the grandstands cheering for one team or the other, the Democrats or the Republicans. The course before us is clear as long as we continue to allow all of our political thoughts to be shaped by the pundits (who are really only corporate employees) on talk radio and on the cable news commentary shows. We watched the Progressive energy that snowballed through the Bush years turn to the massive support of Obama. Now, in looking at the reality of Obama's Presidency (his policies), it is clear that he was a waste of their time and energy. It is clear that the Obama Administration will bring absolutely no noticeable change to our lives. Now we're watching a Tea Party movement turning into nothing but a short-lived Republican revival that will also end in disappointment because the power structure behind it all is the same as it always was. So it goes back and forth, yet only results in more of the same. That's great if more of the same is *what we want*. The thing is, I don't think this is what most patriotic Americans want. To keep on doing that which brings us what we don't want is insane.

It seems to me that we have three divergent paths. On the first path, we can decide that we are happy with the way things are. In this case, we can continue to do as we have done for the past few decades. We can argue theory all day and night about Liberal or Conservative values. We can tell each other how *my* ideas are more right and *your* ideas are crazy. Meanwhile, the reality of the downward spiral in Washington politics just continues in the background almost unnoticed. We can continue to beat ourselves up, or maybe find ourselves giving into despair each time we turn on the news and find that we have lost a bit more faith in the party that we voted for. Maybe we can pray on it. Maybe we can hope that at the end of this spiral is a dramatic rapture. I add this part not out of sarcasm. Real people actually believe this. Who am I to say, for sure, that this may not be what is really happening, right?

Maybe, indeed, we should just continue to reach out to our friends and families as party-line foot-soldiers and try to convince them to vote one way or the other. Maybe we should continue to believe that everything would be ok if it just wasn't for that damn *other side!* We can continue to believe that this game we are watching the President play and the Congress play has anything to do with real life. We can keep telling ourselves that what politicians promise us during the campaign may be real and legitimate (this time). We can keep telling ourselves that the information that comes out publically is the whole story. We can keep on believing that it is possible to change the Republican Party with something like the Tea Party movement. We can keep on believing it is possible to change the Democratic Party from within. We can keep on contributing our hard-earn money to Democratic and Republican candidates in the naïve hope that they will someday represent us. In short, we can do just as we have been for the past few decades. In so doing, we can expect a different result, right?

Maybe you believe that the Libertarian or Tea Party movement is the answer. It might not bother you that it is funded by big business and is an arm of the Republican Party. It might not bother you that your candidates are only saying the exact same things that Ronald Reagan said more than 30 years ago to get elected. This time the outcome will be different, right? You might actually believe, even though you don't believe in government, that when this *next* guy or gal becomes a government bureaucrat he or she is going to somehow drastically cut government to the point where it isn't interfering in your life, to where the budget is balanced, and to where government is no longer a problem. You might ignore the fact that these few people are up against 100,000's of others already in Washington fighting for just the opposite. You might also ignore the fact that

Corporate America seems just fine with the status quo and they have most of the power anyway.

It seems to me that the best chance you have of experiencing the reality of your ideals is to fight hard for the Total Freedom Act. Ask your favorite politician or talk-show host where he or she stands on the Total Freedom Act. Watch his or her reaction carefully. By simply asking the question, we can finally find out whether these influential individuals are sincere about getting government out of our lives. My guess is that they will not support this idea immediately. Right now, the situation is too good for them to want to give up. But this is a reasonable request and it is a battle that can be won.

If indeed, you are a true Conservative and genuinely believe in the free market, I firmly believe that this Total Freedom Act is your most realistic chance to achieve exactly the outcome you desire in your life. We should all remember that what matters most are *our lives*, not what everyone else thinks or does. If you believe that government is the problem, then the Total Freedom Act is the only idea that offers 100% of the outcome you claim to desire. You will never get there as long as you rely on government (hell, you don't even believe in government, remember?).

There is a third path. You might be like me and believe that government *could work* and *should work,* but that ours just *doesn't.* You might understand that the functions provided by government are not just essential, but are completely desirable if we are going to live in a place that is worth living in. You believe that government *can* perform well for us, it just *doesn't.* You know that any government will be far from perfect, but still that a democratic government has the potential to be the best mechanism ever invented to fight for the well-being of *people* over *power.* In a word, you might simply believe in *Democracy.* That's really all I'm asking for – give us true Democracy or give us the option to be free from government. I want the government to be accountable only to the people. That means every decision involves only a consideration of what is best for the people. Anything less than that is something less than Democracy. Exactly how concerned do you think our government is about the people these days?

I guess the only thing to do in that case is to first come to terms with the fact that neither the Democrats nor the Republicans are going to lead us toward a true Democracy and a better government. No other politician supported by big business is ever going to take us there either. We also have to remember that, if a politician is not supported by big business, we will not see this person in the mainstream media. The media is, after all, just another form of big business. They will not let a true pro-people message get out (not if it goes against the interests of the company who owns that media outlet). Ideas that do not support the agenda of the powerful elite will always be framed in a way that it isn't to be taken seriously. They will attempt character assassination and make it look like our side is on the fringe. They will make our candidates seem crazy. Each time they've done that in the past, we've fallen for it, started to believe it, and then started to distance ourselves from the person who is only guilty of being brave enough to speak for us. When they continue to play this card again and again, are we going to continue to apologize for our ideas, continue to distance ourselves from our own movement, and behave just how the powers-that-be want us to? Why? And if we do, then what are our ideas worth?

Any real "people's movement" will also have very little funding to get the message out. But we do have the Internet. There are presumably many people like us. We could stop posting YouTube clips criticizing the mainstream media and calling that activism. We could stop asking institutions to change when they are operating exactly as they intend to. We could stop ourselves from going on and on in despair about how bad the Democrats and Republicans are, how hopeless the situation is, and how we are completely right in theory. You know, we could actually get something done if we could stop being so distracted by the pretty bells-and-whistles in those bright and colorful TV landscapes. I mean, we should stop kidding ourselves that we are fighting for change when all we are actually doing is acting like the guy sitting on the couch bitching about what's on the TV. The ideas and actions we need will not come from a corporation. The ideas and actions we need will not come from any form of media that has any corporate sponsors. The revolution will not be televised! So pay no attention to the commercial media.

I also have a message for so many of the super-educated, purist Progressives who I do respect greatly. But I have to say, you might do well to stop insulting those who think differently from you or haven't come to your exact conclusions yet. You talk a lot about tolerance and open-mindedness and yet you never fail to over-complicate everything and then sneer at anyone who fails to understand…or even happens to be in a different place at the moment (whether that be a person in a different state of mind, or person in a different State from those along the East Coast or West Coast, or even a person who lives in an "un-cool" neighborhood in an otherwise cool city). You might have good intentions and you probably even have some solid arguments backed-up with lots of convincing facts. You probably are really sharp, but sometimes you can act like a real jackass. What good is it when you are right but lose the argument anyway? Doesn't it get tiresome?

I believe there are plenty of Libertarians-at-heart who, after being confronted with the fundamental question posed in this book, will know that they would not choose to opt-out under the Total Freedom Act. They might even begin to question the knee-jerk easy answer that "government is the problem." If you know anyone like this, send them a copy of this book and see what they think of the idea. I know that this book doesn't exactly reflect your values and isn't written in the same tone that you are used to, but what harm can it do if your friends and family start to think of you as a person who does not fit completely, neatly into a box? You don't actually fit into that box. I know you don't. You are a unique individual and the only true value you can bring to this world is exactly that uniqueness.

Regardless of where we stand politically, aren't we proud Americans? Aren't we proud to be descendants of those brave radicals who survived the Wild West, of those great thinkers, those great inventors, those hard workers who came before us? Are we going to be only a hollow shell of those generations, or can *we* become the greatest generation? If so, maybe a good starting-point would be a simple act to restore America as that exception again…that place where pure, true freedom once again can exist. I think we should all like to know that we have this option to opt-out in case something truly terrible happens, like if Sarah Palin becomes President!

I can no longer see any sense in continuing to use moral arguments to legitimize a system that *is amoral* (which ours currently is, right?). In making moral arguments against this idea, you are effectively supporting an amoral institution (the current US Government). Regardless of your opinion on the Total Freedom Act, it isn't anyone's rightful decision to dictate how someone else should choose to live. I have no problem giving people at least the dignity to make their own decisions.

There are still plenty of other people who have spent the last few decades ranting about government as the problem who actually will decide that they *do not want* a life without government in it. Guess what, now we all have a chance to work with these people and start to figure out what kind of government we do want (now that it has been decided that we do, indeed, want a government). We can think about what a pro-people government would look like. We can figure out the basic things government should do in order to play a more positive role in our lives. We, as citizens, can try to find out where we have common ground and we can eventually form some kind of People's Party to start winning elections and getting it done. Maybe that party could be just as anti-Corporate as it is anti big-Government.

This party, this movement, CANNOT accept money from corporations. All support for this movement has to come from all of the people who are sick and tired of Democrats and Republicans. The good news is that there are a lot of us. The bad news is that we have only the streets, the telephone, and the Internet available to us to make this happen. But nothing will ever happen as long as we keep falling for the sweet-talking Democrats, the manipulative and insincere Republicans, or as long as we only support candidates who we agree with 100%. Isn't it good enough that we accept any candidates who are on the side of the people and are prepared to act that way? Perhaps some of these leaders can be Right-wing and some Left-wing, as long as they *fight for the people* and believe that *government can be the solution.* This is going to be such a long-shot. Believe me, corporate America will not stand for it. They will try to destroy us even before we start. We have to be smart. We have to be strong. But we can no longer afford to be as patient as we have been.

I also don't want to say that government is the *whole* solution. Government's role has to be to look out for the people but also to *let the market work.* Government's role has to be to enforce fair rules so that business doesn't cheat and steal from us. Government's role also has to be to allow entrepreneurs the chance to do business (rather than spending all day filling out forms).

But government *does* have to become the people's voice. Everyone should be guaranteed a minimum, basic safety net. The military should only be as large as it needs to be in order to keep foreign powers from invading us and also to handle atrocities around the world (like genocides). Let the market determine the flow of oil and control of resources, not military power. Government's responsibility also has to be to offer every child an equal chance to reach his or her intellectual, creative, and productive potential. The rich already have an advantage. They have a bunch of money. But the rest of us need access to an excellent education, all the way through University, *paid for* through a tax-system where the rich pay their fair share. The government also needs to establish a healthcare system in which *every tax-payer* can go to the doctor without even thinking about money (like in every other country worth living in). Government needs to leave us alone and let us be as free as possible, to enforce laws using only the appropriate amount of force, and to punish convicted criminals using an appropriate penalty. In short, what we need is a government that is formed by the people…a government that will finally have our backs even as big business relentlessly tries to go on doing what it does.

This isn't that complicated! All of this is possible in a country as wealthy as the United States. But it is only possible if the Democrats and Republicans are *pushed into oblivion* by a population that finally gets it! We cannot get scattered! We have watched this same rigged game for at least 30+ years and we keep getting fooled by the same playbook?

I wrote this book because I believe that unless we first address the idea that "government is the problem", nothing that can be said will ever be heard. When the "government is the problem" card is played, all thought immediately stops and only silly ideological arguments ensue. These days, this knee-jerk argument is being used *against everything*! Clearly, it is a perfect way to *shut down thought*! Well, now you have the antidote, in the form of one simple question.

There is only one way I can think of to finally, as Americans, move forward once-and-for-all. The following question needs to be spread far and wide: **If you were offered the chance at total freedom from taxes and total freedom from government in your life, would you take it?**

ABOUT THE AUTHOR

Mark Manney is an American writer, recording artist, and social commentator who uses the alias "Abscondo" to share his ideas across multiple communication channels and art-forms.

Important ideas beg to be shared. Some ideas are best expressed through writing. Since 2004, on the Abscondo Blog, Mark Manney has put together what has become a holistic life philosophy and worldview that connects personal topics such as love, happiness, life purpose, health, finance, and politics. In 2011, Mark also became a published author with the introduction of his political manifesto, Love It or Leave It: The End of Government as the Problem.

Other ideas are best expressed through the emotion of music. Abscondo is a solo musician who released a well-received debut album called Midnight Snow in 2008. In 2010, the artist released a demo EP called Fo(u)r Colors and is currently recording a full-length album.

Still other ideas are best expressed through the dynamics of conversation. Along with his wife Sofia, Mark puts out new episodes of the Abscondo Podcast each week. The show includes honest conversation and interviews with fascinating and accomplished guests. Mark, himself, is also available as a talk-show guest.

Worthwhile ideas must also be compatible with the realities of day-to-day life. Mark is an MBA with more than 15 years of international business experience in the software industry.

Mark Manney is currently located in Eastern Europe; where he lives, works, and creates with his wife and young daughter.